CATTLE
IN AMERICAN HISTORY

NORMAN D. GRAUBART

PowerKiDS press

New York

Published in 2015 by The Rosen Publishing Group, Inc.
29 East 21st Street, New York, NY 10010

First Edition

Editor: Amelie von Zumbusch
Photo Research: Katie Stryker
Book Design: Colleen Bialecki

Photo Credits: Cover Walter A. Weber/National Geographic/Getty Images; p. 4 Worytko Pawel/Shutterstock.com; p. 5 Universal Images Group/Getty Images; p. 6 Dmitry Kalinovsky; p. 7 Oleksandr Lysenko/Shutterstock.com; pp. 8, 18 Science & Society Picture Library/SSPL/Getty Images; p. 9 Cameron Watson/Shutterstock.com; p. 11 MPI/Stringer/Archive Photos/Getty Images; p. 12 Photo Inc/Photo Researchers/Getty Images; p. 13 (top) Izabella Linczer-Katko/iStock/Thinkstock; p. 13 (bottom) muha04/iStock/Thinkstock; p. 14 DEA/G. Dagli Orti/De Agostini Picture Library/Getty Images; pp. 17, 19 Superstock/Getty Images; pp. 20, 21 Monty Rakusen/Cultura/Getty Images; p. 22 tarczas/iStock/Thinkstock.com.

Library of Congress Cataloging-in-Publication Data

Graubart, Norman D.
  Cattle in American history / by Norman D. Graubart. — 1st ed.
    pages cm. — (How animals shaped history)
  Includes index.
  ISBN 978-1-4777-6765-8 (library binding) — ISBN 978-1-4777-6766-5 (pbk.) —
ISBN 978-1-4777-6628-6 (6-pack)
  1. Cattle—United States—Juvenile literature. 2. Cattle—History—Juvenile literature. I. Title.
  SF196.U5G74 2015
  636.200973—dc23
                                    2013048871

Manufactured in the United States of America

CPSIA Compliance Information: Batch #WS14PK5: For Further Information contact Rosen Publishing, New York, New York at 1-800-237-9932

CONTENTS

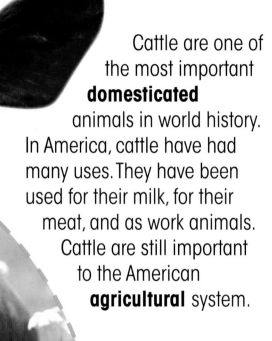

Cattle are one of the most important **domesticated** animals in world history. In America, cattle have had many uses. They have been used for their milk, for their meat, and as work animals. Cattle are still important to the American **agricultural** system.

Male cattle are called bulls, while females are called cows. Babies are called calves.

Over the years, people have created different cattle **breeds**, or types. Some breeds, such as the Holstein and Jersey, are good milk producers. Others, such as the Angus and Hereford, are raised for their beef, or meat. Large cattle trained to work are oxen. Oxen can come from either milk or beef breeds.

Cattle played a big part in the American settlement of the West. Cowboys and cattle are symbols of that period. In this illustration, cowboys help a cow caught in the mud.

ABOUT CATTLE

Cattle are **herbivores**. This means they eat mostly grass and plants. Cattle live in herds. These herds have **hierarchies**. This means that some individuals have more power than others. Usually, older males are the most powerful.

Cows that are raised to make milk are known as dairy cows. They are also sometimes known as milch cows.

When they are outside, cows will eat fresh grass. On big farms, farmers generally feed cattle a mix of corn, hay, soy, and other things.

Female cattle are called cows. Cows have udders that produce milk. Humans have collected milk from cows for several thousand years. Most domestic cows make about 6 to 7 gallons (23–26 l) of milk each day.

Cattle are big. The average cow weighs 1,350 pounds (612 kg). Cattle provide a lot of meat. Meat from young males, called steers, is considered the tastiest.

BRINGING CATTLE TO AMERICA

Settlers brought cattle to the United States from Europe in the early days of **colonization**. The first herd of cattle was brought by the Spanish, who introduced them into the American Southwest in the early sixteenth century. Cattle did not arrive in the British colonies until the early seventeenth century.

Butter is one of several products that early Americans made from milk. It was generally churned by hand, as the woman in this picture is doing.

Jersey cows originally came from Jersey, an island between Great Britain and France. They are one of the oldest breeds of dairy cows.

Both male and female cattle were important in early America. Some steers were trained as oxen and used to pull farm equipment, such as **tillers**. Animals used to pull things are called draft animals. Cows were used for milk. Some of the breeds settlers brought to the colonies were the Jersey, Alderney, and Devon.

Oxen were the most important large animals in early America. They continued to be the most common draft animals until the late nineteenth century. While people used horses to go places, they used oxen to pull farm equipment. Oxen were stronger and less expensive than horses. George Washington even used oxen to haul supplies during the American Revolution!

After the age of four, a steer that cannot breed is considered an ox. In the past, cows were used as oxen, too. Many oxen worked in teams of two. Teams wore **yokes**, which fastened over their necks. Yokes could be attached to carts or plows.

Most of the Americans who settled the West traveled with wagons pulled by oxen. In fact, the guide books of the time recommended using them over mules or horses.

TIMELINE

1493

Christopher Columbus brings cattle to the island of Hispaniola, in the Caribbean.

1848

The Mexican-American War ends with an American victory. The longhorn cattle of southern Texas are picked up by American ranchers.

1450   1500   1550   1600   1650   1700

1784

Rancho San Pedro, the first rancho in California, is granted by Spain.

1869

The Transcontinental Railroad is finished, making it easier to ship cattle without long cattle drives.

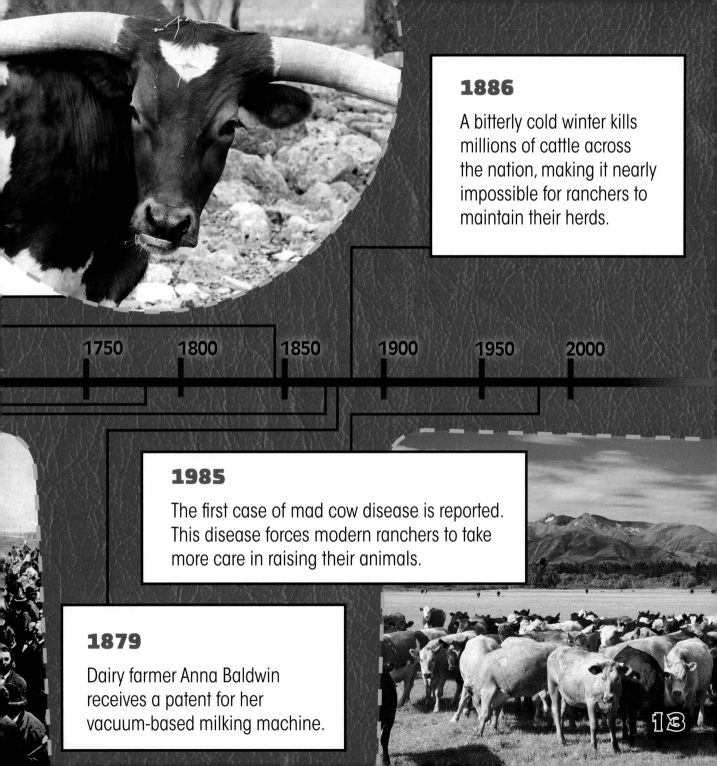

1886

A bitterly cold winter kills millions of cattle across the nation, making it nearly impossible for ranchers to maintain their herds.

1750　1800　1850　1900　1950　2000

1985

The first case of mad cow disease is reported. This disease forces modern ranchers to take more care in raising their animals.

1879

Dairy farmer Anna Baldwin receives a patent for her vacuum-based milking machine.

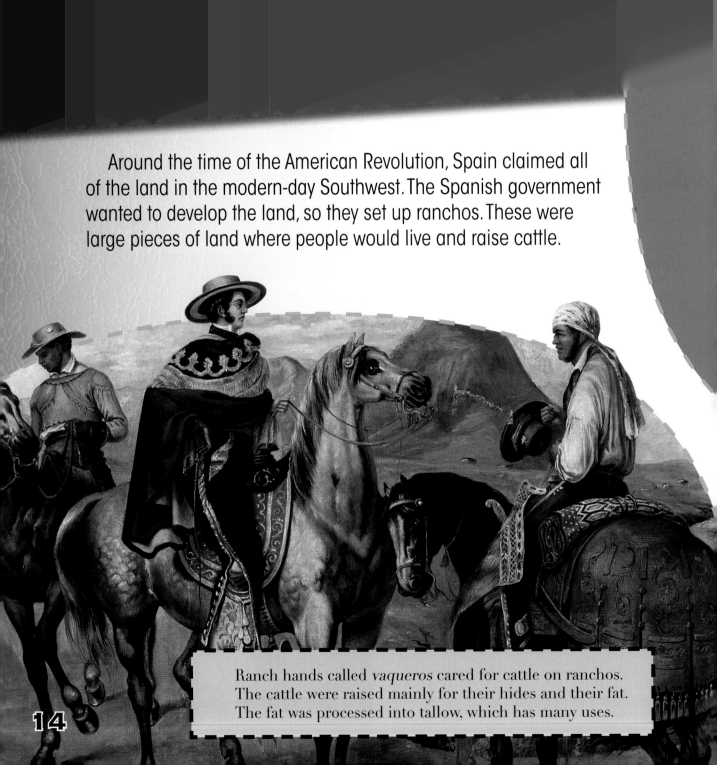

Around the time of the American Revolution, Spain claimed all of the land in the modern-day Southwest. The Spanish government wanted to develop the land, so they set up ranchos. These were large pieces of land where people would live and raise cattle.

Ranch hands called *vaqueros* cared for cattle on ranchos. The cattle were raised mainly for their hides and their fat. The fat was processed into tallow, which has many uses.

Map of the Mexican-American War

United States

Mexican Cession

Texas

Mexico

The Mexican-American War started when American settlers in Texas declared themselves free from Mexico and then joined the United States. The Mexican Cession is what Mexico gave the United States after the war.

Mexico gained independence from Spain in 1821. Mexico continued to give rancho grants to both Native Americans and people from Spanish families. In 1848, the United States defeated Mexico in the Mexican-American War and gained lands in what became the American Southwest. People who owned ranchos were allowed to keep them. As the American cattle **industry** grew around the ranchos, though, they became harder to maintain.

COWBOYS AND LONGHORNS

In the early days of the American West, cattle were held on large, open ranches, where they grazed freely. When the cattle grew old enough, cowboys would round them up and drive them across huge distances to take them to a market. There, the cattle were sold for their meat.

One of the most popular early kinds of beef cattle was the longhorn. Longhorns were cattle that roamed freely in Texas when Americans began to settle there. After railroads were built in the mid-nineteenth century, it became easier to ship large quantities of meat. The Texas longhorn industry grew very big.

This illustration by Charles Marion Russell shows a cowboy roping a longhorn. Cowboys used lassoes, or long ropes with loops at the end, to catch cattle.

17

Trains moved cattle from across the Midwest and West to cities like Chicago. There, the cattle were slaughtered. Beef was packaged and sent to markets all over the country. Many of the people who did this work were **immigrants** who were badly paid.

Cattle were shipped in stock cars. These are railroad cars that have openings in their sides so that the cattle inside can breathe.

Bison hunting was central to the way of life of the tribes that lived on the Great Plains, such as the Pawnees, Crows, Cheyennes, Kiowas, Dakotas, and Blackfeet.

As Americans took over more and more land for cattle ranching, Native Americans began to be forced off of their land. At the same time, bison were being hunted almost to **extinction**. Bison were the main source of food for Plains tribes. This meant that Native Americans had trouble hunting successfully and had to buy beef at high prices.

THE DAIRY INDUSTRY

Milking machines were invented in the late nineteenth century. Before that, farmers had to milk cows by hand. Milking machines were able to get more milk from cows, too. Milking machines are still used today on large dairy farms. Many of them use computers to measure how much milk each cow makes.

Cow milk is used to make yogurt, cheese, cream, butter, and other dairy products. These products used to be made on small farms that had only a few cows. The growth of the cattle industry allowed big companies to make all kinds of dairy products, too.

This is a milking parlor. A milking parlor is the area on a farm to which cows come to get milked.

CATTLE TODAY

Today, most cattle are raised on big farms. However, there are still small farms all over America that have a milk cow that produces milk only for a local market. There are also small ranches that let cattle roam freely and eat grass instead of cattle feed.

Meat and milk are not the only products cows provide. As they did in the past, Americans still make leather from cowhides. Cows are useful in so many ways!

Have you ever seen cows grazing in a field? They are a common sight in many parts of the United States.

agricultural (a-grih-KUL-chuh-rul) Having to do with farms and farming.

breeds (BREEDZ) Groups of animals that look alike and have the same relatives.

colonization (kah-lih-nih-ZAY-shun) The settling of new land and the claiming of it for the government of another country.

domesticated (duh-MES-tih-kayt-ed) Raised to live with people.

extinction (ek-STINGK-shun) The state of no longer existing.

herbivores (ER-buh-vorz) Animals that eat only plants.

hierarchies (HY-eh-rar-keez) Rankings of people, animals, or groups by power.

immigrants (IH-muh-grunts) People who move to a new country from another country.

industry (IN-dus-tree) A business in which many people work and make money producing something.

rancho (RAN-choh) A large farm for raising cattle, horses, or sheep. This term is mostly associated with larger cattle farms.

tillers (TIH-lerz) Tools that prepare soil to grow crops.

yokes (YOHKS) Wooden bars that link two work animals together so that they can pull plows or carts.

INDEX

WEBSITES

Due to the changing nature of Internet links, PowerKids Press has developed an online list of websites related to the subject of this book. This site is updated regularly. Please use this link to access the list:

www.powerkidslinks.com/anhi/cattle/